With God All Things Are Possible!

Copyright © 2016

All rights reserved

ISBN 978-0-9983078-2-4
ISBN 0998307823

All rights reserved. No part of this publication may be reproduced in any means, in any way, without the permission, in writing, from the Copyright owner.   A product of Skookum Books
864 552 1055

Dedication: To the men in my life: my husband Dean, sons, Jim, Steve, Bob, Rick Hargrave, Ned Bixler, Steve Morgan, Jeff Childress, David Wilcox, and Michael Turner! All have taken a piece of my heart, and left behind a treasure trove of goodness in me!

Acknowledgement: I cannot think what my life would have been like without being able to teach all the wonderful children I had! I loved my years of teaching. I loved being with the children and watching them grow and learn many new things! Lois Zank, Earl Hammond, and Bill Beale were my principals who kept me on the straight and narrow and provided all the help a teacher could possibly need!

Skookum Book's Charms

The beautiful butterfly, that graces our flowers and bushes, goes through a mysterious and magical change in becoming an adult! The Greeks believed each time a butterfly emerges from it's cocoon, a new human soul is born! Legend has it that whispering a wish to a butterfly, then releasing it to carry the wish to heaven, will make the wish come true! Perhaps this is when they acquire little clouds on their wings! The butterfly is a symbol of fresh life, happiness, and joy! The "night butterfly", the moth, is attracted to a flame and light, just like our souls are attracted to heavenly truths!

Hummingbirds are active, beautiful additions to our gardens, who give us a sense of life, nature's beauty, and fresh life! These "flying jewels" flit from flower to flower picking up and delivering pollen so that life can continue! It's the creature that opens the heart and shows the truth of beauty. It brings laughter and enjoyment and the magic of being alive! The hummingbird stands for spreading love and joy!

The Ten Commandments
For Teens,
And helpful hints in Between

Betty Lou Rogers

Illustrations by:

Ludovic Nkoth

There are rules that tell us what to do,
And some warning what we should not,
So, don't do what you're not to do,
And, do what you should do, a lot!

For people to work and live in peace,
They must show respect and trust,
Everyone must follow common rules,
That are good, and fair, and just!

God gave these rules to Moses,
Who turned them over to us,
What do we do with all these laws?
"Will we" honor and follow, and trust?

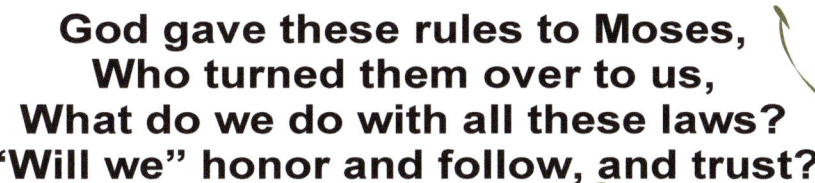

These rules were set so long ago,
To teach, and wisely protect,
They guide us in the way to live,
So we have the life we expect!

Goodness came into our world,
That's peaceful, gentle, and pure,
Be loyal and true to all it means,
'Twill lead to what's right, to be sure!

I. Everyone can have only one God,
You cannot be true to more,
Be it land, or garb, or riches so rare,
Your loyalty will show, for which you care!

Two questions one must always heed,
What is real? What is right?
Beware of leaders who are false,
And run from them with all your might!

II. You must decide who is in control,
Your loyalty must be with only one,
God is first in our hearts and minds,
We must honor Him and His love divine!

What do you think is important?
What do you place first in your life?
Is it goodness, godliness, and brotherhood?
Is it loving God, living the life you should?

You must defend what is good,
You can be tender in caring for others,
You should fight everything that's wrong,
In opposing evil, you must be strong!

III. We should carefully choose which words to say,
Do not use God's name in vain,
Honor our God, by what you speak,
Be honest and humble, and truly meek!

Don't agree with the wrongs in our world,
Don't be a prisoner of greed,
Instead, use all your gifts wisely,
Teach, encourage,--- serve every need!

Humans take care what goes into their mouth,
They want proper nutrition as a rule,
But what spills out of the uncontrolled mouth,
Can be hurtful, ruthless, and cruel!

We should be frank about fairness,
It's what makes our world go around,
Being faithful and keeping a promise,
A better strategy can never be found!

IV. Everyone who works so hard,
And toils for six long days,
The seventh day should be for rest
For renewal, remembrance, and praise!

Love is patient, love is kind,
It's well-mannered from the start,
Love's not jealous or ashamed,
If love is written on your heart!

Love's not selfish, proud, or rude,
Love doesn't tally the times it's used,
It's not shallow, but full of hope,
Love protects, and it will not boast!

V. Love and Honor your parents,
You were given to them, for awhile,
Together, you are a family,
So cherish this privilege with style!

Evil prevents the truth to be known,
Resulting in fighting, chaos, and war,
Evil causes disobedience to parents,
Creating discord and heartaches galore!

VI. It's shameful to have to be told, "do not kill",
Because only One can create a new life,
Those who end a life, have evil hearts,
They cause pain and insufferable strife!

Now, in dealing with other people,
Be it family, or friends, or new folks,
You never, not ever, cause tension or tears,
For much trouble you'll surely provoke!

VII. You should treat your neighbor as a friend,
And show loving care, and concern,
You should not want what your neighbor has,
But be happy for what they have earned!

If ever you feel unhappy with life,
Because of your wishes for more,
Hard work is one way to discover what's true,
Happiness can't be bought in a store!

▥ VIII. Another rule says, do not steal,
That means, take nothing from others,
It's a very selfish and lazy endeavor,
Looks like you can't manage without Mother!

And when you grow weary, and full of doubt,
You want to be someone worth noting,
So what do you do, when you feel so defeated?
"Treat others the way you'd like to be treated!"

IX. Weigh the words that you choose to say,
Be honest and stay with the truth,
Don't dirty your mouth with ugly words,
Keep yourself a well-controlled youth!

Liars "toy" with all the facts,
And use words like a game,
They tell such tales, for all to hear,
To win themselves some fame!

They promise this and promise that,
They care not what they claim,
Instead of holding up their heads,
They should hang them down in shame!

Don't be a weak-minded person,
Shun wickedness and wrong, senseless deeds,
Be willing to fight for peace in our world,
Your changed life, will help you succeed!

X. We all have things that we treasure,
They were earned by working all day long,
But when we see others possessions,
And want them as well, then it's wrong!

When people boast they love to help,
Then they show you, they care not at all,
A hypocrite is what you see,
Whose worth to anyone, is very small!

Many think tolerance is a wonderful act,
But it really is a non-caring word,
Because you're only "putting up with" differences,
Which makes your "righteousness" absurd!

So, rather than "put up with" some people,
You could love them, and show them you care,
You can overcome problems with kindness,
Encourage, be patient, and fair!

Don't surrender yourself to what's shameful,
Don't become a slave to the master of hate,
Many burdens are caused by such actions,
Instead, find the happiness that awaits!

When someone is full of anger,
They hate everything that's good,
They bring harm and hurt, and lack the love,
That leads to peace and brotherhood!

We were meant to be joyful, not sad,
We were meant to be free, not enslaved,
We were meant to be hopeful, not burdened,
We were meant to be strong and be brave!

So, be happy with those who are happy,
Be humble and don't be too proud,
Be joyful and share with all others,
Use your gifts to serve all as allowed!

Forgive and forget is the way to live,
Join all together, don't divide,
Be merciful, with true understanding,
keep kindness close by your side!

To those so-called thugs in our world,
Who torture, and kill, and maim,
They do not know the value of life,
Their evil will rot, our love will remain!

We need a world that cares for all,
We need love instead of violent acts,
True love, it-self, cannot be stopped,
It conquers all, and that's a fact!

God gave these rules to Moses,
Who turned them over to us,
What do we do now with these laws?
We "should" honor, and follow, and trust!

If you want to make others feel worthy,
And show them you really do care,
Just light your face up with a sunny smile,
And send friendly greetings, everywhere!

So-o-o-o-o

There are rules that tell us what to do,
And some warning what we should not,
So, don't do what you're not to do,
And, do what you should do, a lot!

And always remember, never forget - - -

America is your homeland,
'Twas won with blood and strife,
And cherish all our freedoms,
And guard them with your life!

About the Author

Betty Lou Rogers is a retired fourth grade teacher from Madison Elementary School in Sandusky, Ohio. Her strategy for success was simple. Engage! Work together! Be active learners! Then employ her "one more chance" philosophy! Betty Lou Rogers grew up in rural northwestern Ohio, graduating from Fremont Ross High School. She married her childhood sweetheart and raised three sons. During this time, she returned to college where she graduated with a B. S. Degree in Elementary Education from Bowling Green State University, in Bowling Green, Ohio. She was a member of the prestigious educational society, Kappa Delta Pi. While teaching at Madison School, Mrs. Rogers was keenly aware of what children needed, both as a group and as individuals, in effectual learning in the classroom. She also had the intuition to know how to accomplish this by challenging her students to be active learners, as opposed to the sit, listen, and absorb approach! Always have lesson material in front of the student, so they are actively participating in the lesson, never pushing the child beyond their ability, but always working toward the best they can do! Often times the student is awakened to and surprised by their own ability. Mrs. Rogers' most telling educational approach was offering the children "one more chance" to learn and succeed, by giving open-book tests!

Tests show what the student hasn't learned! "My job is to give the children every opportunity to learn." This strategy caused her students to become more familiar with the contents and location of information in their books. This offering, enabled them to find the answer, complete the test, and learn what was missed before. These answers could even be more meaningful to them! When parents found this out, there was no excuse for a failing grade!

Mrs. Rogers was also a Jennings Scholar, which honored and rewarded teachers in the elementary classroom. The Jennings Foundation provides a means for greater accomplishment, on the part of teachers, with the hope it would result in greater recognition for those in the teaching profession within the public school system. Mrs. Rogers is a member of Advent United Methodist Church in Simpsonville, S.C. Besides writing, she loves her sewing and crafts, and gardening! Mrs. Rogers and her husband have four granddaughters, and seven great-grandchildren!

After twenty-seven years of teaching, Mrs. Rogers philosophy for success has permeated the American landscape through her students in both academic and professional fields. Her love for teaching and writing, can never be equaled in any way, except her hope for students to find her writing truly illuminating!

Mrs. Rogers' previously published works:

The Thimseagle Thievers
Change Can Be Good!
Paste and Gluey, A Sticky Tale!
New publications coming:
Kate Earns Her MBA in Manners, Behavior, Attitude!
Chris Earns His MBA in Manners, Behavior, Attitude!
A new series of books for preteens and teens:
It's So Important To Be Honest!
The Ten Commandments for Teens, and Helpful Hints In-Between!
Proverbs, The First Book Written For the Young, Plus A Little Bit For Everyone!
Acquiring The Human Skills of Thinking, Saying, and Doing, for Teens!
A Medley of Options for the "Not Yet Old" Set!
God and Country. Two Sets of Laws For Teens!
The Human Dilemma of the Young, The Scramble for PAM! Power, Approval, and Money, (Ecclesiastes)
A Hodge-Podge of Thoughts For Teens, That's Not Gibberish!
Law and Order for Teens: Ignore or Restore!
ABC's For Teens, and What They Mean!
So, You Think We Shouldn't Have Dropped "The Bomb"?
For fun: Bossy Susie Saucy   and Capricious Caleb O'Connor

www.ingramcontent.com/pod-product-compliance
Lightning Source LLC
Chambersburg PA
CBHW041230040426
42444CB00002B/116